BOB MARLEY

Vicky Shipton

D0110561

LEVEL 3

■ SCHOLASTIC

Written by: Vicky Shipton

Publisher: Jacquie Bloese

Editor: Fiona Davis

Designer: Dawn Wilson

Picture research: Pupak Navabpour

Photo credits:

Cover: Idols/Photoshot.

Pages 4 & 5: P Mazel/LFI/Photoshot; Ron Laytner; E Roberts, D Corio/Redferns, M Ochs Archives/Getty Images; AP/Press Association Images; L Seco/iStockphoto.

Pages 6 & 7: A Boot/56 Hope Road Music; D Pearson/Corbis.

Pages 11 & 13: E Leonelli/Photoshot; I Keeman/Redferns/Getty Images.

Pages 14 & 15: Popperfoto/Getty Images; Mary Evans Picture Library; D Walker, M Bondarchuk/iStockphoto.

Pages 16 & 17: J Black, www.urbanimage.tv; E Anderson/Corbis.

Pages 18 & 20: A Boot/56 Hope Road Music/www.urbanimage.tv.

Pages 22 & 23: H Guttmann/Hulton Archive Getty Images; M Trommer/iStockphoto; Gallo Images/Alamy

Pages 25, 26 & 27: M Ochs Archives/Getty Images; Jamaway/Alamy; AP/Press Association Images; Jzunino/iStockphoto.

Page 29: A Messers/Rex Features.

Pages 32, 34 & 35: PictorialPress/Alamy; AP/Press Association Images; Mirrorpix.

Pages 36 & 37: I Dickson/Rex Features; E Roberts/Redferns/Getty Images.

Pages 38 & 41: A Webb/Magnum.

Pages 44, 46 & 47: E Roberts, D Corio/Redferns/Getty Images; P Jordan/Alamy.

Pages 49, 51, 53 & 55: M Prior/Redferns/Getty Images; Sipa/Rex Features; Zuma, F Stark/Alamy; L Seco/iStockphoto.

Pages 56 & 57: daboost, K Kulikov, narvikk/iStockphoto; F Stark/Alamy.

Pages 58 & 59: P LeSegretain, J Dyson, D Livingston, S Hussein/Getty Images.

Pages 60 & 61: M Cameron/Redferns, D Hogan, R Scherman/Getty Images.

Published by Scholastic Ltd. 2013

Mary Glasgow Magazines (Scholastic Ltd.)
Euston House
24 Eversholt Street
London NW1 IDB

Printed in Singapore

CONTENTS   PAGE

BOB MARLEY

Bob Marley was born in Jamaica in 1945. With his band The Wailers, he introduced reggae music to millions of people all around the world. Years after his death in 1981, people still listen to his music and his message of peace.

Bob's father, 'Captain' Norval Marley

Bob's mother, Cedella Marley Booker, with Bob's wife, Rita (r), and Bob and Rita's daughter, Cedella (l) in 1994.

In the early 1960s,
Neville 'Bunny' Livingston (l),
Bob Marley (c)
and Peter Tosh (r)
formed **The Wailers**.

Bob Marley and the Wailers
in 1977. The I-Threes,
including Rita (in the red scarf),
were singers with the band.

PLACES

Bob spent his early years in Nine Miles – a little country village in the north of Jamaica.

Trench Town

Trench Town is the poorest area of Jamaica's biggest city, Kingston. Bob and his mother moved there when he was twelve.

56 Hope Road

This is the house in Kingston where Bob lived when he became famous.

It was a warm summer night in 1975. Thousands of people had come to London's Lyceum Theatre. Not everyone had tickets for that night's gig and some people tried to climb into the hall through the roof! They were all here to see the Jamaican singer and songwriter, Bob Marley, and his reggae band, The Wailers.

The next night's gig was sold out too. The band's record company recorded the Lyceum gigs and produced one of the greatest live albums ever.

Soon millions of people around the world loved the music of Bob Marley and the Wailers. But becoming rich and famous were not the most important things for Bob Marley. He had a message that he wanted to share with the whole world through his music. Some of his songs told Jamaicans and black people to fight for their rights. But he also sang for everyone in the world to come together in peace.

CHAPTER 1
Country boy

St Ann, Jamaica

Cedella 'Ciddy' Malcolm was born in 1926 in Nine Miles, a small village in a beautiful hilly area of northern Jamaica called St Ann. Like many Jamaicans in the country, she worked on her family's farm as soon as she was old enough. Her father, Omeriah, was an important man in the area and the family was not poor. But life on the farm meant long, hard days and as a teenager, Ciddy wanted something more exciting in her life. She found it when she met Norval Marley.

'Captain' Marley – as he was known – was a white man who worked for the Jamaican government. It was his job to help more Jamaicans farm the land in St Ann. Every month Marley rode his horse to St Ann for work and he stayed with the Malcolm family. Soon Omeriah helped him build a little wooden house to stay in. Marley became very friendly with Ciddy. Although Marley was much older than her – some people say he was in his fifties and she was just eighteen – Ciddy liked the attention and fell in love with him.

Soon Ciddy had some news for her father. She was pregnant with Marley's baby. Omeriah was angry, not only about the age difference, but also the fact that 'the Captain' was a white man. In the 1940s, Jamaica was still under British rule and white people and black Jamaicans did not mix much. It was said that Marley's family did not respect black Jamaicans. And some black Jamaicans did not like the fact that Ciddy was pregnant by a white man. Omeriah was worried about his grandchild's future.

When Marley rode to the farm and asked Omeriah if he could marry Ciddy, Omeriah agreed. He thought his daughter and grandchild would now have a better life. Ciddy and Marley were married on June the 9th, 1944. But it was not the start of a happy life together. Soon after the wedding, Marley left for Kingston. He told Ciddy that he needed an easier job in the city. Ciddy stayed in St Ann to have her baby. Marley did not return for a long time, although he sent some money to his wife.

On February the 6th, 1945, Ciddy had a baby boy. His skin was light in colour and Ciddy decided to call him Robert Nesta Marley. It was a name that showed his mixed family history. Robert was the name of his white father's older brother. Nesta was a black Jamaican name.

Robert's early years in Nine Miles were happy. Later in life he said, 'I come from country and country is always good.' However, he almost never saw his father. Then, when Robert was just six years old, his father suggested taking him to Kingston. He wanted to pay for him to go to a good school. Although Ciddy was not happy to lose her son, she wanted the best for him and so she agreed.

For a year, Ciddy heard no news of her son. During this time she was busy with her new business, a small general shop in the village of Stepney, near Nine Miles. But then a friend came back from Kingston with a worrying story. She had seen Robert in the city and he was living with an old woman called Mrs Grey. Ciddy went to the city and learned the truth. Robert's father had taken him to the old woman's house. He had promised to return soon, but the boy never saw his father again. Now Robert was living with the old lady and doing jobs around the house to help her. He went to school in the city, but not all the time.

Ciddy took her son back to live with her in St Ann. Every day Robert walked home from school and helped his mother in the shop. He was happy to be back near his family. He was a hard-working boy, who was quiet but popular. He loved to play football with his friends. Music was a big part of his life too. It was important for all the Malcolm family: Ciddy liked to sing old church songs around the house, and the family often met at Omeriah's farm to make music. Robert's cousin, Nehemiah, even made Bob his first guitar.

Ciddy's shop was not a success. She decided to sell it and look for work in Kingston. She left Robert with his grandfather on the farm. Omeriah made his grandson feed the animals and work on the land. Later, Robert remembered this as a happy time, but life was not perfect. With his lighter skin, Robert did not look like anyone else in the village. Some people in the village said that Robert worked twice as hard as everyone else. Was he trying to show that he was just as good as everyone around him?

For a while Robert was sent to stay with his mother's sister, Amy, several miles from the rest of the family. Robert's aunt expected him to get up at five o'clock in the morning to do hours of work before school. It was too much for Robert. He packed his things and ran away, all the way back to Nine Miles. After that, Amy refused to let the boy back in her house. Ciddy realised that it was time for a change. Their future was in the city now. And so in 1957, at the age of twelve, Robert was put on the bus for Kingston. His time as a country boy was over and a very different part of his life was just beginning.

CHAPTER 2
Trench Town and the first record

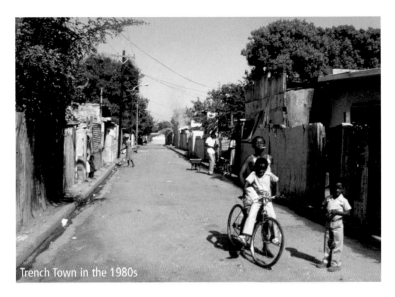

Trench Town in the 1980s

Ciddy wanted to give her son a better future. However, the schools in Kingston were either too expensive, or she didn't think they were good enough. Robert went to a number of schools and he and Ciddy lived in several small flats in the city. Finally they moved to an area of Kingston called Trench Town.

In Trench Town, Bob – as he was now known – still faced problems because of the colour of his skin. Some people asked why he was here in Trench Town instead of the richer parts of the city where white people lived.

Bob's mother had a boyfriend now, Toddy Livingston, a man who she knew from St Ann. Toddy already had a family, but he quickly became angry if Ciddy spoke to another man. Bob did not like his mother's friendship with Toddy. However, because of him, Bob became much

LIFE IN TRENCH TOWN

Trench Town was one of the poorest areas of Kingston. In the 1950s, the government had built lots of flats there. The people had to share kitchens and toilets. With no wind from the coast or the mountains, Trench Town could be unpleasantly hot. However, many people remember the area as a friendly place to live. Later Bob Marley sang about his early life in Trench Town.

But life in Trench Town was often difficult. In the 1970s, the area became more and more dangerous. There was little money and few jobs, and some people turned to crime. Young men who spent a lot of time on the streets were called 'rudeboys'. Like Bob Marley, many of these had moved from the country to the city. With little work to be found, many rudeboys were angry with the government.

closer to an old friend from St Ann, Toddy's son, Neville 'Bunny' Livingston. The two boys loved to sing and make music together. Bunny showed Bob how to make his own guitar from a large, empty fish can.

In 1960, when Bob was fifteen, he decided to leave school. He told his mother to give his school books away. He wanted to earn money from music instead. Ciddy did not believe that there was a real chance of this, and so she found her son a job. Bob learnt how to weld. He did not really enjoy this work, but through it he met some people who became important to his music. Desmond Dekker was a welder too, but he had also made a record which was played on the local radio. Through Desmond, Bob met Jimmy Cliff, another successful singer at the time, and Leslie Kong.

Kong had a shop where he sold ice cream and records. He was also a producer with a small record company called Beverly Records. When he heard Bob sing, Kong agreed to produce his song 'Judge Not'. The song was in

Desmond Dekker, 1967

the style of ska – fast dance music that was very popular in Jamaica at the time.

Kong did not pay much – just ten Jamaican dollars for a song – and he decided to change Bob's last name on the record to Martell! This did not matter to the fifteen-year-old Bob, who walked home proud of his record. The only problem was that neither Bob nor any of his friends had a record player!

Bob's early records were not hits. He started to play gigs in the city and sometimes he entered music competitions. In later years, Bob was amazing on stage, but in these early days, crowds did not always like him and sometimes shouted for him to leave the stage.

Although Bob was not yet successful, he believed that a musical future was possible. He saw music as a way out of Trench Town, but more than this he just loved to play and sing songs. He left his welding job and worked just on his music. But he was no longer happy with Leslie Kong and Beverly Records. It was time for a change, and for that Bob needed a little help from his friends.

A HISTORY OF JAMAICA

The Arawak and the Spanish

The Arawak people from South America were the first people to arrive on Jamaica. They lived on the island peacefully from around the year 650.

Everything changed in 1494 when Christopher Columbus arrived. He was the first white European to step on the island. War and illness killed many of the Arawak people, and the rest became slaves of the new Spanish rulers. It was the start of the island's long history of slavery.

The Spanish began to bring slaves to Jamaica from countries such as Angola in the south-west of Africa.

Life was terrible for these black Africans. They were far from home and they had no rights.

Jamaica and the British

In 1655 the British took Jamaica from the Spanish. But life for the island's slaves became no better. The British brought more slaves to work on the island's sugar and coffee farms. In the eighteenth century around 600,000 African slaves were brought to the island. Many more were sent from Jamaica to other islands and to the Americas.

Britain finally ended slavery in 1834. Black Jamaicans were free, but their

Slaves working at a Jamaican sugar factory in 1849

country was still under British rule. After more than 300 years of slavery, the people of Jamaica had to build a new country and way of life. Most people on the island were black and terribly poor. Rich white Jamaicans from British families still held most of the important jobs.

Independence

After World War II, many countries got their independence and were not now under the rule of European governments. Jamaica stayed under British rule until 1962, when Bob Marley was seventeen. During the twentieth century, many Jamaicans left the island and moved to countries like the UK and the US to find a new life.

Jamaican immigrants arriving in the UK, 1954

CHAPTER 3
Bob, Bunny and Peter: The Wailing Wailers

Growing up in Trench Town, Bob and Neville became friends with an older boy called Winston McIntosh – later known as Peter Tosh – who shared their love of music. Peter was already a good guitarist and he even owned a real guitar. His skill on the guitar pushed Bob to practise harder. Sometimes Bob stayed up all night practising.

Bob (l), Peter and Bunny (r)

The three young men played together all the time and decided to form a band. They discussed different names for the band. At first they called themselves The Wailing Rudeboys but they soon changed this to The Wailing

Wailers. ('Wail' means 'cry'. They used this name because of the hard lives of the people of Trench Town.)

A local musician, Joe Higgs, helped them and gave them advice. They often played popular American songs of the time and listened carefully to find out which songs people liked best. The band practised in local parks and on street corners. Joe even told them to play at night in the local cemetery. If they were brave enough to play in a cemetery at night, they were brave enough to play on stage! For two years, the band practised with Joe Higgs' help, before they finally went to see a record company, Studio One.

Studio One was owned by Clement 'Coxsone' Dodd, one of Jamaica's 'systems men'*. Coxsone was said to be a hard man who did not always pay his musicians enough money. But, in Bunny Livingston's words, Coxsone 'knew when the sound was right'. The sound of Bob, Tosh, Bunny and another friend, Junior Braithwaite, was certainly right for the times.

Bob with Clement 'Coxsone' Dodd

* See page 18.

THE SYSTEMS MEN

In the early 1960s, many people in Jamaica were too poor to own record players or radios. But people loved music and wanted to hear new songs. The answer was the systems men. The systems men drove around the country with huge sound equipment on their cars. They used to stop somewhere and play records. Lots of people came and there was a huge dance outside. The systems men played an important part in Jamaican music at the time.

The band recorded their first song for Studio One in 1963. It was a ska song that Bob had written called 'Simmer Down'. This song was a message to Kingston's rudeboys to avoid crime. Jamaica was no longer under British rule. Jamaicans were excited to be living in a free country, but life had not become easier for the poor in Kingston. Too many young people had turned to crime.

'Simmer Down' was very popular in Jamaica and sold around 80,000 copies. However, like most musicians in Jamaica at the time, The Wailing Wailers earned very little money from the record. The band's success continued, but they had not yet found their true style. Like many Jamaican musicians, The Wailing Wailers were following the style of American bands. They dressed in smart suits like American singers and sometimes they even sang their own versions of the same songs.

Around this time, Bob's mother, Ciddy, had a child by Toddy Livingston. Now Bob and Bunny shared a half-sister, Pearl. Bob also became a father himself when his girlfriend had a baby girl, Imani Carole. Bob was still only seventeen years old. Soon Ciddy made an important decision. She had relatives in Delaware in the US, and she decided to try and find a better life there. Her plan was to move there and then send for her children after three months.

When she left, Ciddy wanted Bob to stay with relatives in Kingston, but the young man had other ideas. He was busy recording and writing songs for Studio One and now he began to sleep at the studio. Always serious about music, he helped any group that came to record. For this help, he received just three dollars a week.

Bob and his band often walked through Trench Town to Studio One. One morning a teenage girl shouted to them. Her name was Alvarita Anderson – Rita – and she enjoyed singing with her cousin and a friend. Together they sang in the style of Motown, the most popular African-American music at the time. Born in Cuba, Rita had moved to Kingston as a young girl. Like Bob, she was living in the city without her parents – her mother and father had moved to Britain. When Bob and his band heard Rita and her friends sing, they told them to go to Studio One. Coxsone liked them and he immediately wanted the three singers at his studio.

Rita Marley, 1980

The three singers called themselves The Soulettes and they sang with The Wailers. Bob was a quiet, serious man and at first Rita did not think that he was interested in her. But that soon changed and the two became boyfriend and girlfriend. Rita's aunt even built a little room at the side of her house for Rita and Bob to live in together.

Three years after she left, Bob's mother was now ready for her children to come and live with her in the US. Ciddy had married again – she was now Ciddy Booker – and lived with her new husband in Wilmington, Delaware, on the East Coast. Now Bob had to decide what to do about his future. He had become less and less happy with Studio One. Coxsone still paid his musicians hardly anything for records, even successful ones. Bob decided to try life in the US, but he wanted to marry Rita first. They were married on February the 10th, 1966. Bob was twenty-one years old. Like his own father, Bob said goodbye to his wife soon after the wedding and left.

In the US, Bob found several jobs and worked in a car factory for a while. He earned more money than he could in Jamaica, but he was not happy. Often he stayed at home, playing his guitar and writing new songs. He just wanted to earn enough to go back to Jamaica and start his own record company. Then he received a letter from the US government. It said that he had to go and fight in the Vietnam War*. Instead Bob flew back to his wife in Jamaica with $700 in his pocket and a lot of new songs.

* The Vietnam War (1954–1975) was between North and South Vietnam. The US supported South Vietnam.

CHAPTER 4
The rise of reggae

When Bob came back to Kingston, Bunny and Tosh were still making music as The Wailers. Rita was waiting for Bob, and she had lots to tell him. In April, 1966, Haile Selassie I, the Emperor of the African country of Ethiopia, had visited Jamaica. Selassie believed that all the black people of Africa should come together. But for some people in Jamaica, Selassie was much more than just a political leader, he was the living god of the religious movement, Rastafari.

Crowds in Kingston wait for Haile Selassie I to arrive.

There were many Rastas in Trench Town and Bob had spent time with them before he left for the US. The ideas of the movement were attractive to him. As a child of

RASTAFARI

Rastafari is a religious movement that started in Jamaica and grew from Christian beliefs in the 1930s. Rastafarians, or Rastas, believe that the true word of God, or Jah, was a message to the many black people around the world whose families had been taken from Africa as slaves. To Rastas, Africa is their true home. Many Rastafarians believe that Haile Selassie I, who became Emperor of Ethiopia in 1930, will one day lead his people back to their true home. The movement takes its name from Selassie's name before 1930, Ras Tafari.

Rastafarians follow a way of life which they take from the Bible. They do not believe in cutting their hair and usually wear their hair in long dreadlocks or dreads. The lion is an important animal in Rastafari. Long dreadlocks look like a lion's hair. Rastas do not usually eat meat and drink no alcohol, but they use the drug marijuana. They say that it brings them closer to Jah.

The Rastafarian colours are red, green and gold. Black is important too.

 Red is for the slaves who lost their lives in the fight to be free.

 Green is the colour of the natural world and a sign of hope.

 Gold is for the riches of the homeland, Ethiopia.

 Black is the colour of the African people.

mixed race, Bob had never felt at home in either world, black or white. A central belief of Rastafari was that no black people outside Africa were 'at home'.

It is hard to say if Bob called himself a Rasta before he went to the US. Certainly, he had begun to explore the ideas of the movement and its way of life. After Selassie's visit, Rita became a strong believer in the Rastafari movement and from this time, Bob's music also showed the growing importance of his Rastafarian beliefs. The message that all people should live together in peace was always there in the words of his songs.

When he arrived back from the US, Bob could finally start his own record company. It was called Wail'n Soul'm* and was named after the two bands, The Wailers and The Soulettes. Musical tastes in Jamaica were changing. Now instead of ska, the slower dance style of rocksteady was more popular. The Wailers' first new record 'Bend Down Low' was in this style. Radio stations did not play the record much at first, but the band took records to dance halls themselves on bicycles! The plan was a success and the song was a hit. The band continued to be very popular in Jamaica. In October, 1967, their song 'Stir It Up' was another hit.

However, money was still a problem for the band. With a child for Rita and Bob on the way, The Wailers left Trench Town and moved to St Ann. The plan was to save money and live a simple life by working on the land. For a while, Bob and Bunny were happy to be back in the country. Peter Tosh found it harder – he was certainly not a country boy! He missed having a TV and an electric light to read by. Rita also missed Kingston and did not want to have her baby away from the city.

* Wail'n Soul'm later became Tuff Gong International.

The Wailers moved back to Kingston and Bob and Rita's daughter, Cedella – named after Bob's mother – was born on August the 23rd, 1967. The following year the couple had their first son. His name was David, but they called him Ziggy.

Around this time, The Wailers were looking for a new producer and they found someone who made a big difference to their music. Lee 'Scratch' Perry had once worked for Coxsone, but he left to start his own record company, Upsetter. Scratch had a group of musicians who he always worked with. The Barrett brothers were an important part of this group – Aston 'Family Man' Barrett played bass guitar and his brother, Carly, played drums. With Scratch producing and the Barrett brothers playing, the Wailers had begun to find a new sound in their music. This sound was reggae.

The Wailers, c. 1970

THE BIRTH OF REGGAE

The people's music

In the 1920s and 1930s the most popular kind of music in Jamaica was called mento. Mento took some European musical traditions and added African or Caribbean rhythms and drums to make something new. Jamaicans called it 'the people's music'.

Ska and rocksteady

In the 1950s, many young Jamaicans were listening to American music on the radio. Then ska music arrived. It was a mix of popular American music with some Caribbean traditions of mento. It was fast, exciting and good to dance to! Ska became even more popular after Jamaica got its independence in 1962. Young Jamaicans were proud of their own music. But ska bands at the time – like The Skatalites – often still recorded ska versions of famous US and UK songs. The Wailing Wailers recorded ska versions of songs by The Beatles and Bob Dylan!

A new sound

After ska, Jamaican musicians moved towards a slower style of music called rocksteady. But the time was right for a new kind of Jamaican music. People disagree about who first gave the world

The Skatalites playing in 2007

Snoop Lion (in sunglasses) with three of Bob Marley's sons, including Ziggy (l)

reggae. The style of music first appeared in Kingston around 1968. Some people think that the tradition of Rastafari African drumming played a part. Certainly, The Wailers were one of the first groups to explore this new style and most people agree that they were the best too.

Other early reggae artists included Bob's old friends from his welding days, Desmond Dekker and Jimmy Cliff. In the 1970s, reggae artists such as Burning Spear and Black Uhuru had strong political messages.

Reggae styles

Over the years Jamaican reggae has changed. The drums and bass guitar are very important in dub reggae. Songs from a later style called dancehall are usually about life for young people in the city. Some people think the words are too violent.

Today reggae is still popular. Jamaican artist Sean Paul has successfully mixed reggae with hip hop and other styles. In 2012 the American rap artist Snoop Dogg recorded a reggae album in Jamaica, using the stage name Snoop Lion.

> **What do these words mean? You can use a dictionary.**
> tradition   rhythm

CHAPTER 5
'Catch A Fire'

In the early 1970s, more and more people were listening to the music of The Wailers. The band made two reggae albums with Lee 'Scratch' Perry, *Soul Rebels* (1970) and *Soul Revolution* (1971). They recorded some songs for CBS, a large international record company, and travelled to London. But the trip did not go well. Bob felt that CBS were not supporting The Wailers or doing much to make their music popular. There were several problems and finally CBS ended plans for a UK tour. The Wailers found themselves in London with no money.

London was the home of the record company Island Records, and Bob decided to go and talk to them instead. It was 1973 and Chris Blackwell at Island Records was waiting to find the company's next big star. He was a fan of reggae, but Island's biggest reggae star, Jimmy Cliff, had left. When Bob and the band came into his office in London, Blackwell knew that his search was over. He offered the band £4,000 to make a new album. It was a lot of money to The Wailers. Blackwell also wanted to change the band's sound so that rock fans would like it too. He remembers that Bob was happy about the offer. However, the other Wailers were not so sure.

The Wailers went back to Jamaica to make the album. When *Catch A Fire* was finished, Bob flew to London to give the songs to Chris Blackwell. Blackwell then mixed and produced the record again, adding some rock guitar. Marley did not mind, but he asked for a different *Catch A Fire* album – one without Blackwell's changes – for the Jamaican market. Most people agreed that the album was the band's strongest collection of songs yet.

LISTEN TO ... 'STIR IT UP'

'Stir It Up' was Bob Marley's first successful song outside Jamaica. American singer Johnny Nash had a hit with this song in 1972. On *Catch A Fire* the band recorded the song again and it soon became one of Bob Marley's most famous songs.

People in the music business were excited about the album. Blackwell sent the band on a tour of the UK to win more fans. In some ways, it was like starting again – in Jamaica The Wailers were stars, but in the UK they had to play in small concert halls. The purpose of the tour was to introduce the album to as many people as possible, so the band still did not earn much money from it. Bob did not dislike life on the road – the hours on the tour bus, the different food, the colder weather – but the others were less happy about it.

On tour in the UK in 1973

Bunny Livingston's Rastafarian beliefs were very strong. Life on the road made this difficult for him. When Blackwell asked the band to tour the US, Bunny decided not to join them. Joe Higgs, the band's old teacher from their early days in Trench Town, took Bunny's place on the US tour.

Sometimes The Wailers played with other more famous singers and bands. At one gig in New York City they played to a crowd that had come to see the young Bruce Springsteen! They also played with the band Sly and the Family Stone, but they were soon dropped. Some people said that the band's leader, Sly Stone, dropped The Wailers because they were too good!

LISTEN TO ... 'GET UP, STAND UP'

Bob wrote one of the most famous songs on *Burnin'* about the poor people of the island of Haiti. It was a strong message for them and for people everywhere to stand up for their rights.

Like many of his songs, it also included lines about Bob's Rastafarian beliefs. When he sang 'God is a living man', he was singing about Haile Selassie.

Things were moving fast now, and the band recorded another album in 1973, *Burnin'*. It was another great collection of songs. The band's success was growing, but not everyone was happy. Peter Tosh did not really like Chris Blackwell and Island Records. In Tosh's opinion, Blackwell did not let the band make enough of their own decisions. He left the band saying, 'I need respect.' Bunny finally left the band too. The three old friends who had practised and practised in Trench Town were no longer together.

LISTEN TO ... 'I SHOT THE SHERIFF'

'I Shot The Sheriff' on the *Burnin'* album, tells the story of a man who has killed someone to save his own life. The song was later recorded by rock guitarist and singer Eric Clapton and introduced Bob Marley to rock fans around the world.

CHAPTER 6
56 Hope Road

Back in Kingston, Bob needed a new place to work. Chris Blackwell of Island Records owned a beautiful building in a very expensive part of the city, Hope Road. Blackwell allowed Bob and the band to use the house at 56 Hope Road. When Bob and the band first arrived there, the (mostly white) neighbours were not very happy. Bob and his friends were the first Rastas to live in this part of the city. But Bob loved 56 Hope Road. It was a huge house with lots of rooms for the band to practise and for people to come and stay.

Bob brought in new musicians, including Rita (in red).

For the next album – *Natty Dread* – Bob brought in new musicians to take Bunny and Tosh's places. Bob also brought in three female singers, called the I-Threes. One of these singers was his own wife, Rita. There was another change to the band: they were now called Bob Marley and the Wailers. It was very clear to everyone now that Bob was the leader. The album *Natty Dread* had another strong mix of religious and political messages. There were also personal songs on the album. The new band toured around the world, and the album was another success.

LISTEN TO ... 'NO WOMAN, NO CRY'

One of Bob's most famous songs first appeared on *Natty Dread*. In it he sings about good times with friends back in Trench Town. He sings about sitting together in the government yards, the shared areas of Trench Town's buildings.

On the album the name V. Ford is listed as the song's writer. This was an old friend of Bob's from Trench Town. Many people think that Bob really wrote the song himself, but wanted his friend to have the money from it.

The band recorded a live version of 'No Woman, No Cry' at their famous gig in London's Lyceum Theatre. The live version became a huge hit, and most people know it better than the version on *Natty Dread*.

Bob was now able to buy 56 Hope Road and he was becoming more and more comfortable there. Usually he did not go out to see people. Instead they came to Hope Road. There were always lots of people there, discussing politics and religion. Bob and Rita had three children now – Stephen was born in 1972 – and they lived with Rita in a smaller house a few miles away.

When the band practised at Hope Road, Bob wanted them all to follow his rules. Because of his Rastafarian beliefs, women could not wear make-up, and they had to wear dresses, never trousers. Exercise was very important to Bob. In the morning, the band often went for a run along the beach or into the mountains. When they were not practising songs, they often played games of football outside 56 Hope Road. After music, football was Bob's great love, and he always wanted to win.

Bob Marley playing football in 1980

Although Rita sang in the band, she played a smaller part in Bob's personal life now. She still looked after their children, but Bob saw other women. For a while he lived with an actress called Esther Anderson, who he had met in London. Now, in Hope Road, Bob noticed another woman, a light-skinned Jamaican called Cindy Breakspeare. She was quite famous because she had won some beauty competitions. She later entered the Miss World beauty competition as Miss Jamaica. The competition was held at the Royal Albert Hall in London and it was watched all over the world. Cindy won and later she spoke to reporters about her Rasta boyfriend, Bob Marley. The two were close for the rest of his life, and had a child, Damian, together.

Cindy Breakspeare, Miss World, 1976

Life at Hope Road continued, but in 1975 there was sad news for all Rastafarians. Haile Selassie – the man who was a living god to Rastas – died in Ethiopia at the age of 83. His death was terrible news for his followers. Some Rastafarians refused to believe that he was really dead.

Bob gave no interviews about Selassie's death. However, for his next album, *Rastaman Vibration*, he wrote a peace song called 'War'. This song used words that Haile Selassie himself spoke to the United Nations in 1963 on the subject of Africa and its future. Soon Bob's message of peace was needed closer to home, when Jamaica faced one of the most difficult times of its history.

FAMILY AND CHILDREN

Bob and Rita had an unusual marriage. Rita already had a child, Sharon, when she first met Bob. Bob thought of Sharon as his own child. Bob and Rita had three more children together, Ziggy, Cedella and Stephen, and Rita stayed with him until the end.

At times, Bob and Rita did not live together. Bob sometimes told people that he was not married. He saw many other women and several had children by him. Bob had at least eleven children by seven different women. The mothers of these children were known as Bob's 'baby mothers' and Rita knew all about them. Sometimes she even looked after the children as part of her own family.

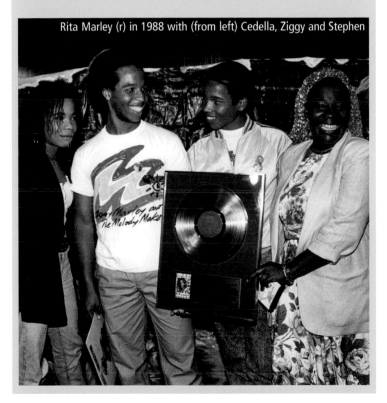

Rita Marley (r) in 1988 with (from left) Cedella, Ziggy and Stephen

CHAPTER 7
Guns at Hope Road

In the 1970s, Jamaica's problems had continued to grow. There was not enough money or work for its people. There were two main political parties. The PNP (People's National Party) was the country's government and Michael Manley was the Prime Minister. The other main party was the JLP (Jamaica Labour Party), whose leader was Edward Seaga. The two parties had very different political ideas, and the disagreements between the supporters of both parties soon became violent. Jamaica had become a very dangerous place to live. In 1976, the violence was so bad that the government brought the army onto the streets of Kingston.

Kingston, 1976

Bob had strong political beliefs but these were very general. He just wanted his country to stop the violence and find peace. He did not support one leader or the other and he had friends from both parties. So when Prime Minister Michael Manley asked him to play a concert to help end the violence, Bob agreed. Plans were made for the 'Smile Jamaica' concert.

After Bob agreed to play the concert, the government showed photos of him at Michael Manley's house. Bob was angry – he was not doing the concert to support the PNP. Next, Bob learned that Manley planned to give the country a vote for a new government right after the concert. Again Bob did not want to look like Manley's supporter. But he knew that the violence had to end.

Bob and the band began to practise for one of their most important gigs ever. As usual, they practised at Hope Road. Two days before the concert, the band had finished for the night and they were sitting in the kitchen. Suddenly the door opened and a hand in a dark glove appeared. It was holding a gun. The gunman began to shoot. Bob's manager fell, and then Bob felt a terrible pain in his chest and in his arm.

Outside the house, Rita was already in her car, ready to drive home to the children. Another gunman started shooting at her. Two gunmen came to check on her. Blood was coming from her head and they thought that she was dead. Before they left into the night, Rita heard one of them say, 'Everyone's dead.'

December 1976

BOB MARLEY SHOT

Luckily the gunman was wrong. Bob and Rita were taken to hospital. There were several other injuries, but nobody died. Neither Bob nor Rita's injuries were very bad, but everyone was scared. Who had ordered the shooting? Nobody ever found out.

The Marley family was taken to a safe house. But the big question was, should the band still play the 'Smile Jamaica' concert? Did the gunmen plan to come to the concert and shoot again? Rita did not want to play, but Bob wanted to send a message to the gunmen. They could not stop him from playing for the people of his country.

On December the 5th, 1976, over 80,000 people waited in the National Heroes Park in Kingston to hear Bob Marley and the Wailers. Nobody knew if Bob would appear. When the band finally came out on stage, the crowd shouted their support. There were almost 200 people on stage to protect the band but nobody tried to shoot Bob again. The concert was a huge success. Although Bob was unable to play the guitar because of his injury, the band played for over ninety minutes. Bob even showed the crowd his injuries. The crowd loved him for it.

Bob singing at the 'Smile Jamaica' concert

After the concert, Bob did not want to stay in Jamaica. Instead he moved to London and started working on a new album. The band lived together in one big building in

Chelsea, a very expensive part of London. Each musician lived on a different floor of the house. It was a happy time. Bob was glad to be alive after the shooting, and he worked harder than ever. He was only sleeping for around four hours a night, and he expected The Wailers to be ready to play at any time. When the band was not practising, they enjoyed playing football in a London park.

In 1977, the new album came out. By now, Bob Marley was an international star. *Exodus* was a huge hit in the UK and it included some of Bob's best and most famous songs. In the Bible, the Exodus was the time when the Israelites left Egypt to find their homeland. For Bob, the word meant the return of black people everywhere to the homeland of Africa. In general, the album showed a softer side to Bob and his music. One of the album's songs, 'Jammin'', became a huge hit. In Jamaican English, this word means getting together with friends.

LISTEN TO ... 'THREE LITTLE BIRDS'

One of the most popular songs from Exodus was 'Three Little Birds'. Some people say that Bob wrote the song about three birds that he used to watch in the mornings at Hope Road. Others say that he often called the I-Threes his 'three little birds'.

Exodus was Bob's biggest hit yet, and a concert tour could only make the album more successful. But when it was time to tour the US, there was an unexpected problem. Bob had a pain in his big toe after a game of football. Doctors gave him tests. There was terrible news.

Bob had cancer. The doctors said that they needed to cut the toe off. Bob could not believe this. If he lost the toe, how could he play football? How could he dance on stage? He spoke to more doctors. Finally one doctor told him that he did not have to lose all of the toe, just a small part of it. Bob agreed to this and a few months later he was back on tour. He did not know it at the time, but the doctor had given him the worst possible advice.

CHAPTER 8
'One Love'

Bob and the band recorded a second album in London in 1978. When people heard the album, *Kaya*, some said that Bob's music was going soft. But for most fans, the songs about love showed a different side of Bob's music.

LISTEN TO ... 'IS THIS LOVE'

'Is This Love', from the album *Kaya*, is one of Bob's most personal and romantic songs. In this love song, he seems to be remembering his early life in Jamaica.

While Bob was recording these albums in London and finding new fans around the world, Jamaica's political problems continued to grow. Since the 'Smile Jamaica' concert, the violence between the two political parties had become worse than ever. Every day there was gun crime between supporters of the two parties on the streets of Kingston. Normal life had become impossible.

By 1978, the leaders of both political parties knew that the country could not continue in this way. They were ready to discuss peace. But after so long, could they stop the violence now? They knew that the people of Jamaica would listen to Bob Marley. So they each sent someone to London to ask him to return. If Bob would play another concert – a peace concert to bring the country together – perhaps it would bring an end to the violence.

Knowing how important this concert was, Bob said yes. It was called the 'One Love' peace concert. When Bob returned to Jamaica, thousands were waiting for him at the airport. Tens of thousands more came to see the concert. Old friend Peter Tosh agreed to join the band on stage too. Many people remember that night as much more than just a concert. There was a real feeling of happiness as everyone came together. Supporters of the PNP and the JLP stood side by side in the crowd. The most famous moment of the evening was one that Bob had not planned. He called for Michael Manley, the leader of the PNP, and Edward Seaga, the leader of the JLP, to join him on stage. With the music still playing, Bob joined the two men's hands in the air. Of course, Jamaica's political problems did not end that night. But the message was clear to everybody there – sometimes music could even bring enemies together in peace.

Bob holds the hands of Michael Manley and Edward Seaga (r) on stage.

Bob started living back at Hope Road, and more and more people visited him there. Long lines of people stood and waited to see him. Many of them wanted help and money, and Bob was generous to them all.

Outside Jamaica Bob had become a huge international star. When the band toured Europe, they played to huge crowds. But Bob had begun to worry that most of the people at these concerts were white. He wanted to reach black fans outside of Jamaica. As usual, Africa was never far from his thoughts.

The band recorded the next album, *Survival*, back in Kingston. When it came out in 1979, people saw that Bob's songs had become more political again. In one of the songs – 'Zimbabwe' – he sang about African politics. At that time in southern Africa, black Africans were fighting to free their country, Zimbabwe, from years of British rule. These fighters took hope from the words of Bob's song and its promise to 'fight for our rights'.

The next year Bob played a gig in Africa for the first time. He was invited to play in the city of Libreville in Gabon. He was happy to be playing in Africa at last, but this was not a happy trip in other ways. At first Bob did not know that they were playing a concert for a political dictator. He then discovered that his manager had not told him the truth about how much money the band was earning from the concert.

Bob's next trip to Africa, later the same year, was more successful. British rule was finally over in Zimbabwe. The new government and its leader, Robert Mugabe, invited Bob to play a concert. Bob was so excited that he did not want to receive any money for the concert and paid to send all the band's equipment there himself.

Zimbabwean people celebrating independence, 1980

The date of the concert was August the 18th, 1980.
Bob was surprised by the crowd that waited for him. At
the front there were important politicians from the new
government and from around the world. The rest of the
people were supporters of the new government. But many
people who supported a different political party were
not allowed in. These people waited outside. When they
heard the music start, thousands of them tried to push
their way inside. There were too many people and it soon
became dangerous.

Suddenly the band heard screams from the crowd. The
police had begun to use tear gas to drive the crowds back.
On stage the musicians' eyes and throats began to burn.
Rita and the other singers ran from the stage, frightened.
The other musicians soon followed until only Bob was
on the stage. Finally he too had to leave. But when his
eyes stopped burning, he returned to the stage and sang

'Zimbabwe'. It was a great moment for him. The next evening he put on another concert for the people who had been unable to see him the night before.

After Zimbabwe, the band toured Europe again, this time breaking all records for crowd numbers. More than one million fans saw the gigs in twelve European countries. The new album, *Uprising*, had come out that year and it was another big hit. Bob was reaching more people than ever with his music.

Bob Marley in London, 1980

LISTEN TO ... 'COULD YOU BE LOVED'

'Could You Be Loved' was one of the big hits from *Uprising*. This happy dance song was quite different from Jamaican reggae. Some fans thought that it was the closest that Bob ever came to pop music.

Perhaps the most unusual song on *Uprising* was the last one. When Bob gave him the record, Chris Blackwell asked him for one more song to finish the album. Bob went away and recorded 'Redemption Song'. It was different from anything he had ever sung before. This amazing song was not reggae, and Bob played it and sang alone. It was the sound of a man looking at the meaning of his own life.

Although the European tour for *Uprising* was a big success, Bob still worried about one thing. Most of his fans in the US were white. He had not reached the African-American market. To change this, he agreed to open a concert for the American band The Commodores in New York City. His manager thought that this was crazy. Bob Marley and The Wailers were bigger stars around the world than The Commodores. But Bob wanted to reach new fans in the US.

The concert went fantastically well. The crowd danced and sang to all of the songs. It was clear to Bob now that they could bring African-Americans to their music. After the concert, he was excited about the rest of the US tour. But then something happened that changed everything … .

CHAPTER 9
'Don't Give Up The Fight!'

In September, 1980, Bob Marley and the Wailers were in New York and ready for the band's biggest US tour ever. One morning Bob went out for a run in New York's Central Park with a friend. During the run he fell in sudden pain. He was shaking all over. His friends took him to the hospital, but once more there was terrible news. The doctors had not been able to kill the cancer. Now it had moved around Bob's body. The doctors said that they could do nothing to help him. In their opinion, Bob had around three months to live.

But Bob had a strong body and a strong personality. He decided to fight the illness and continue the tour. The next show was in the city of Pittsburgh. However, when Bob joined the band for the sound check before the concert, something was clearly wrong. They played just one song, again and again, for over two hours. It was a song that had a new meaning for Bob now – 'I'm Hurting Inside'.

The band played the Pittsburgh gig on September the 23rd, 1980. It was a great show, but the people in the band could see that Bob was not feeling well. At the end of the gig, the crowd shouted for more. The Wailers were worried. Was Bob strong enough? But Bob came out and played four more songs. Then, when the crowd shouted again, he went out on stage once more. Nobody knew it, but this was Bob's goodbye to playing live. The Pittsburgh gig was his last time on stage.

Bob spent his last months in and out of hospitals as doctors fought to save him. He lost his famous dreadlocks and began to cover his head with a hat at all times. Finally the American doctors decided that they could do no more to help. But Bob was still trying to fight the cancer. He flew to a special hospital in the south of Germany and lived there for eight months. His German nurse remembers him as patient and friendly – she called him 'Bobby'. In the winter 'Bobby' walked through the snow to reach the hospital every day. He felt a long way from sunny Jamaica.

On Bob's 36th birthday, family and friends flew to Germany to be with him. Bob was still holding on to his hopes – he had sent a message to his fans saying, 'I'll be all right.'

However, Bob's illness was getting worse and finally all hope was gone. In May, 1981, he flew to Miami. He had hoped to get back to Jamaica, but it was not possible. Rita brought his children to see him in the hospital there. He spoke to his children and told them goodbye. To Rita he said, 'I'll be with you always.' Then, on May the 11th, 1981, Bob Marley died.

The news was met with terrible sadness all over Jamaica. His body lay in the Ethiopian Church in Kingston. Thousands of people came to say goodbye. On the day of his funeral, the whole country stopped. During the funeral, Rita and his daughter, Ciddy, read from the Bible. His two sons, Ziggy and Stephen, danced on the stage. People all around the world watched the funeral on television.

Bob Marley's body was taken back to St Ann. On the way, thousands of people stood in the streets wearing the black, green and gold colours of Jamaica or the red, gold and green of the Rastas. At last his body was brought to the village of Nine Miles. Bob Marley was back home.

Crowds wait to welcome Bob Marley home to Nine Miles.

At times in his early years, Bob Marley was very poor, but when he died, he had around eight million dollars. But it was not the money that was important to Bob. A reporter once asked him if he was rich. Bob answered that he was rich in the love of the people around him.

There was one more new Bob Marley and the Wailers album for his fans. *Confrontation* had been recorded during Bob's last times in a studio. The album came out in 1983. A year later, Island Records brought out *Legend*, a collection of Bob Marley and the Wailers' best songs.

LISTEN TO ... 'BUFFALO SOLDIER'

The most famous song on *Confrontation* was another hit around the world. Bob sings about a black man 'stolen from Africa, brought to America'.

Today Bob's music lives on around the world. His music is still hugely popular, and every year new fans are introduced to it. To many people, reggae music *is* Bob Marley. Reggae fans can also listen to the music of his children. Many of Bob's children have become musicians. Bob's oldest son, Ziggy, formed the band The Melody Makers with Stephen, Cedella and Sharon when they were still children. The band made several albums before Ziggy started to record alone. In 2012, Ziggy recorded a live album. On it he sang two of his father's most famous songs, 'Is This Love' and 'War'. Damian Marley, Cindy Breakspeare's son, is a musician too. Like his father, he is also a Rastafarian.

Ziggy Marley

Bob's children have recorded music together and they sometimes get together to play gigs. On September the 23rd, 2010, some of his children and his wife, Rita, played a concert of his songs in Pittsburgh. The 'Live Forever' concert was thirty years after his last gig there.

Bob's daughter, Cedella, now runs his recording studio. Tuff Gong International is one of the largest recording studios in the Caribbean and supports young Jamaican musicians. Tuff Gong Pictures is also a film production company. Their film about Bob's life, *Marley*, was an international success. The film came out in 2012, the same year that Jamaica celebrated fifty years of independence.

LISTEN TO ... LEGEND

Legend was produced by Island Records and was the record company's most successful album ever. It is the best-selling reggae album of all time and has sold around twenty-five million copies worldwide.

Above all, Bob Marley is remembered for the message in his songs. This went further than his Rastafarian beliefs about Africa and the future of black people. It was a message for everyone to stand up and fight for their rights. It was a message of togetherness for all the people of the world.

JAMAICA

**Bob Marley lived in Jamaica for much of his life.
What is life like in Jamaica today?**

A Caribbean island

Jamaica is a large island in the Caribbean Sea, south of Cuba and west of Haiti. The island is 235 kilometres from east to west. It is only 82 kilometres across at its widest point, but there is a lot to see there. There are mountains, rivers, forests and, of course, beaches. Jamaica's largest mountain is Blue Mountain, in the east of the island.

The hot weather brings many tourists to the island. But Jamaica can also be hit by hurricanes from the Atlantic Ocean.

The people of Jamaica

Almost three million people live on the island. Over 91% of these are black – they are mostly the descendants of slaves brought to the island from Africa. Through the island's history, people from many other nations have come to Jamaica and added to the mixed population. The country's motto is 'Out of many, one people'.

Most people on the island speak English or a mix of European and African languages called Jamaican *patois*.

Kingston

What are the best things about your country? Does it have any problems?

Trouble in the city

Just over half the population of Jamaica lives in cities. Kingston is the capital city with over 900,000 people. There are still a lot of poor people – around 14% of the Jamaican population has no work.

Crime continues to be a problem and Kingston is one of the most dangerous cities in the world. In 2011, there were over 500 murders there. The Jamaican government is working hard to end the country's illegal drug business.

Montego Bay

The Jamaican economy

Jamaica still exports coffee, sugar and fruit to the rest of the world. But the country's most valuable export is bauxite. This is used to make aluminium.

The island receives most money from the tourist business. Tourists from other countries usually avoid Kingston and go to the smaller city of Montego Bay, where there are beautiful beaches and expensive hotels.

What do these words mean? You can use a dictionary.
hurricane   descendant   motto   illegal   economy   aluminium   export

Usain Bolt

FAMOUS JAMAICANS

Everyone knows that Bob Marley was born in Jamaica, but the tiny island has produced many famous people.

Usain Bolt For such a small country, Jamaica produces a huge number of top athletes. Born in 1986, Usain Bolt is one of the greatest sports people of all time. At the Beijing Olympics in 2008 he ran in the 100-metre and 200-metre races. He won gold and broke the world record in both races. Four years later he won gold in the same races at the London Olympics. But in magazines, Usain has said that he is 'lazy'!

Grace Jones is a singer, model and actress. She spent her early life in Jamaica, but moved with her family to the US at the age of seventeen. Grace recorded some dance hits for Island Records, such as 'My Jamaican Guy' and 'Slave to the Rhythm'. She has also acted in several films, including the James Bond film *A View to a Kill*.

Grace Jones

Jamaican roots

Many Jamaicans moved from their island home to the US, Canada or the UK, where they brought up their children.

will.i.am is one of the most successful artists in modern music. He is a singer, songwriter, rapper and producer. will.i.am sings with The Black Eyed Peas but he has also had hits on his own and with many other artists. Will was born in a poor area of Los Angeles in the US. After he became successful, he bought new houses in a better part of the city for all of his family.

will.i.am with his mum, Debra

Naomi Campbell is a top model and very proud of her Jamaican roots. Naomi's Jamaican mother moved to London, and Naomi was born there. Naomi worked with Bob Marley when she was just five years old – she was in Bob's video for the song 'Is This Love'. Naomi started modelling at the age of sixteen and is one of the most famous models in the world.

Who is the most famous person from your country at the moment? What are they famous for?

What do these words mean? You can use a dictionary.
athlete   roots   bring up   rapper   model

59

Naomi Campbell

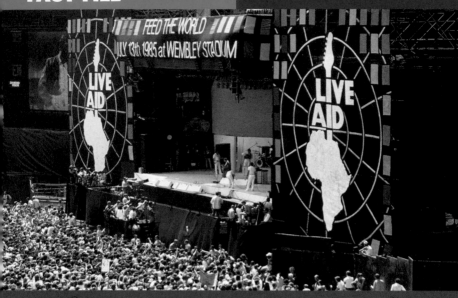

The Music and the MESSAGE

Bob Marley used his music to tell the world about his strong beliefs. Many other musicians have used their music to help others or change the world for the better.

Live Aid

In 1984, the world saw terrible news from the African country of Ethiopia – millions of people there were starving.

British pop stars Bob Geldof and Midge Ure wanted to help. They wrote the song 'Do They Know It's Christmas?' and recorded it with top pop stars of the time. One of the singers was Bono from the Irish rock band, U2. The charity record with its strong message sold over 3 million copies.

The following year there was a concert called Live Aid. Live Aid took place in both London, in the UK, and Philadelphia, in the US. It lasted for over sixteen hours and around 1.9 billion people watched on television around the world. The concert raised around £150 million.

ONE and 46664

Bono from U2 helped to start ONE, a group which wants to end poverty around the world. Bono has also met international leaders and won their support.

In South Africa in 2003, Bono sang with Beyoncé at the first 46664 charity concert. The 46664 charity takes its name from Nelson Mandela's prison number. Nelson Mandela fought for the rights of black people in South Africa and was put in prison for twenty-seven years. The charity continues his work and beliefs.

The first 46664 concert raised money to support work in Africa against AIDS. Since 2003, there have been several concerts around the world.

John Lennon

The famous singer with The Beatles, John Lennon, saw music as a way to bring peace. His song 'Imagine' asks people to imagine a world with no religion, politics or countries.

Beyoncé

Beyoncé supports many charities and her songs have a strong message. She wants to help the lives of young women around the world. With songs like 'Run The World', she hopes to teach young women everywhere 'to be strong'.

> **Which songs do you know that have a clear message?**

What do these words mean? You can use a dictionary.
starving   raise   poverty   charity   AIDS

CHAPTERS 1-3

Before you read

You can use your dictionary.

1 Complete the sentences with these words.

**an album   a competition   a gig   a new version   a producer
a stage   a studio**

a) ... works with musicians to record songs.

b) A musician plays in front of fans at ... .

c) ... is usually at the front of a theatre.

d) ... is a record with several songs by a musician or group.

e) Musicians make records in ... .

f) This is ... of a Beyoncé song – its's great!

g) She's a good singer – she won ... .

2 Look at 'People and places' on pages 4–5. Name the places.

a) Bob Marley was born in this country.

b) Bob lived in this village when he was a child.

c) Bob moved to this part of Kingston.

d) Bob lived in this house when he was famous.

After you read

3 Are these sentences true or false? Correct the false sentences.

a) Ciddy Malcolm was from a big city.

b) Captain Marley and Ciddy were the same age.

c) Ciddy and Captain Marley got married.

d) Robert was happy in Nine Miles.

e) Robert's father took him to Kingston.

f) Trench Town is a rich area of Kingston.

g) The Wailers recorded their first record at Studio One.

4 Complete the sentences with these names.

Desmond Dekker   Clement Dodd   Neville Livingston   Peter Tosh

a) ... was known as Bunny.

b) ... had a recording studio.

c) ... knew how to weld.

d) ... owned a real guitar.

CHAPTERS 4-6

Before you read

You can use your dictionary.

5 Complete the sentences with these words.

bass   drugs   drum   support

a) A criminal was selling … in the area.

b) I … my country's football team.

c) The child made a lot of noise on his toy … .

d) A … guitar plays low notes.

After you read

6 Put these events in the right order.

a) The Wailers travelled to London.

b) Bunny and Peter left The Wailers.

c) Haile Selassie visited Jamaica.

d) The Wailers had a hit in Jamaica with 'Stir It Up'.

e) The band met Lee 'Scratch' Perry.

f) The band recorded their first album with Island Records.

g) Bob Marley started the Wail'n Soul'm record company.

7 Answer these questions

a) Where was Bob and Rita's daughter, Cedella, born?

b) What was the name of their first son?

c) Which two American singers had hits with Bob Marley songs?

d) Who was 'Get Up, Stand Up' written for?

e) Who died in 1975?

f) What competition did Cindy Breakspeare win in 1976?

8 Tick the sentences that are true about Rastafarianism.

a) Red, green and gold are important colours. ☐

b) Rastafarians think that Jamaica is their true home. ☐

c) They follow a way of life which they take from the Bible. ☐

d) They cut their hair often. ☐

e) It started in the 1930s. ☐

9 What do you think? What part did Bob Marley and the Wailers play in the history of reggae?

CHAPTERS 7–9

Before you read

You can use your dictionary.

10 Match the definitions with these words.

cancer   funeral   tear gas   violence

a) A time to remember someone who has died.

b) An illness which can kill.

c) This makes it hard for people to see or breathe.

d) This sometimes happens between supporters after a football game.

11 What do you think? Look at the title of Chapter 7. Why were there guns at Hope Road? Now read and check.

After you read

12 Match the events with the concerts.

a) Police fired tear gas.

b) There were 200 people on the stage to protect Bob.

c) This was Bob's last time on stage.

d) The leaders of two political parties joined Bob on stage.

i) 'Smile Jamaica', 1976

ii) The 'One Love' peace concert, 1978

iii) Zimbabwe, 1980

iv) Pittsburgh, 1980

13 Complete the sentences with these places.

Germany   Miami   New York   Nine Miles   Pittsburgh

a) When he was in … , Bob fell ill with cancer.

b) He flew to a special hospital in … .

c) Bob Marley could not get back to Jamaica, but died in … .

d) Bob Marley's body was brought to … .

e) Thirty years after his death, Rita and some of Bob's children played the 'Live Forever' concert in … .

14 What do you think? 'Bob Marley was more than just a musician.' Do you agree with this statement? Why / Why not?